PENGUIN CLASSICS

NOTHING ... EXCEPT MY GENIUS

OSCAR FINGAL O'FLAHERTIE WILLS WILDE was born in Dublin in 1854, the son of an eminent eye-surgeon and a national-ist poetess who wrote under the pseudonym of 'Speranza'. He went to Trinity College, Dublin, and then to Magdalen College, Oxford, where he began to propagandize the new Aesthetic (or 'Art for Art's Sake') Movement. Despite winning a double first in Classical Honour Moderations ('Mods') and the Newdigate Prize for Poetry, Wilde failed to obtain an Oxford Classical Fellowship, and was forced to earn a living my lecturing and writing for peri-odicals. He published a largely unsuccessful volume of poems in 1881 and in the next year undertook a lecture tour of the United States in order to promote the D'Oyly Carte production of Gilbert and Sullivan's comic opera *Patience*. After his marriage to Constance Lloyd in 1884 he tried to establish himself as a writer, but with little initial success. However, his three volumes of short fiction, *The Happy Prince* (1888), *Lord Arthur Savile's Crime* (1891) and *A House of Pomegranates* (1891), together with his only novel, *The Picture of Dorian Gray* (1891), gradually won him a reputation as a modern writer with an original talent, a reputation confirmed and enhanced by the phenomenal success of his society comedies, *Lady Windermere's Fan*, *A Woman of No Importance*, *An Ideal Husband* and *The Importance of Being Earnest*, all performed on the West End stage between 1892 and 1895.

Success, however, was short-lived. In 1891 Wilde had met and fallen extravagantly in love with Lord Alfred Douglas. In 1895, when his success as a dramatist was at its height, Wilde brought an unsuccessful libel action against Douglas's father, the Marquess of Queensberry. Wilde lost the case and two trials later was sentenced to two years' imprisonment for acts of gross indecency. As a result of this experience he wrote *The Ballad of Reading Gaol*. He was released from prison in 1897 and went into an immediate self-imposed exile on the Continent. He died in Paris in ignominy in 1900.

OSCAR WILDE

Nothing ... Except My Genius

Compiled by ALASTAIR ROLFE

With an introductory essay, 'Playing Oscar', by
STEPHEN FRY

PENGUIN BOOKS

PENGUIN BOOKS

Published by the Penguin Group
Penguin Books Ltd, 27 Wrights Lane, London w8 5TZ, England
Penguin Putnam Inc., 375 Hudson Street, New York, New York 10014, USA
Penguin Books Australia Ltd, Ringwood, Victoria, Australia
Penguin Books Canada Ltd, 10 Alcorn Avenue, Toronto, Ontario, Canada M4V 3B2
Penguin Books (NZ) Ltd, Private Bag 102902, NSMC, Auckland, New Zealand

Penguin Books Ltd, Registered Offices: Harmondsworth, Middlesex, England

This compilation first published 1997
'Playing Oscar', by Stephen Fry, first published in the *New Yorker* 1997
7 9 10 8

Typeset in 10.25/12.5pt PostScript Monotype Fournier
Designed in Quark XPress on an Apple Macintosh
Printed in England by Clays Ltd, St Ives plc

Contents

Playing Oscar

A few years ago, I sat for the British artist Maggi Hambling as she painted a series of portraits of me. Not long afterwards, she embarked on a series of drawings and sculptures of Oscar Wilde, and, as it happened, I was asked to play Wilde in a film of his life. Hambling, who has the true artist's ability to be simultaneously earthy and mystical, played with the coincidence by doing a series of drawings in which I 'morphed' into Wilde. She has a very high and real sense of Wilde's importance to artists everywhere and was delighted at my good fortune, just as I was delighted when, a year later, she won a competition to create the first statue of Wilde to be erected in central London. I couldn't help feeling a tinge of envy, however. While I am not suggesting that to make a statue or a painting of Wilde is easy – far from it – the materials an artist uses allow a kind of displacement, a passionate, engaged objectivity that is denied an actor. I was going to have to use my voice, my face, and my body. No wax, bronze, oils, or acrylics for me – just my own befuddled self.

'Playing Oscar' could be the title for as hellishly postmodern and self-reflexive a game as was ever devised. To pose as Oscar Wilde, the author of 'The Truth of Masks', a man perceived by many (myself often included) to be posing as one who posed at being a poseur – how many

Chinese boxes in a hall of how many mirrors does that make?

The first rule, I have discovered, when embarking on such a project is to block your ears and lock up all mail-boxes, real or electronic. Letters arrive. Oh, how letters arrive.

Dear Mr Fry, I hope you will not be forgetting that the key, the only key, to Oscar is that he was and is, first and foremost, *Irish* ...

Dear Mr Fry, Wilde's works whinny and shiver with Victorian gay underground codes. Do not shirk the force of his sexual identity ...

Dear Mr Fry, Wilde's love of his wife and family is consistently overlooked by biographers. I trust you will not fall into the same error ...

Dear Mr Fry, Wilde's lifetime yearnings towards Roman Catholicism are central to any understanding of ...

Dear Mr Fry, I draw your attention towards Wilde's *Soul of Man Under Socialism*. Oscar's unique brand of libertarianism is scandalously overlooked by contemporary ...

Dear Mr Fry, Oscar Wilde was in reality a woman. This secret was passed on to me by my grandfather, who had a lesbian affair with her in Bad Ischl, June 1897 ...

Dear Mr Fry, It is a little-known fact that Oscar Wilde did not die in 1900 but in 1962, after pursuing a successful career in theatre and the electric cinema under the name Charles Laughton ...

Dear Mr Fry, Oscar Wilde's soul entered my body on 9 August 1963 ...

Dear Mr Fry, Oscar Wilde and the Marquess of Queensberry were in reality one and the same man ...

I have spared you the weird ones.

*

If I were to say that all my life had been a preparation for playing Oscar Wilde, I would (aside from sounding ridiculous) be laying my tender rear horribly on the line. Yet I had been made to feel for years that this might be true. I have had archly nudged into me the winsome phrase 'born to be Wilde' more times than I care to remember. 'The chubbier you get the more you look like him,' I have been told. 'If you can't, no one can.' And 'Let's be honest. With a face like yours, it's the only lead you'll ever get. Otherwise, it's a life of Gestapo interrogators, emotionally constipated cuckolds and Bond villains.'

It is certainly true that even if I had never been an actor I should have always felt drawn to Oscar Wilde. However, knowing that I was to play him; reading and rereading his works and the endless catalogue of Wildeana that surrounds him and his circle; listening to so many voices inside and outside my head telling me who he was, what he was, and why he was; and entering debates on hair, gait, accent, laugh, favoured cigarette, average daily alcohol intake, and sexual position of choice – all this turned the six months that preceded Day One Principal Photography into a period of slightly trippy disengaged fever.

Disengaged because our project, *Wilde*, was a British

film, which meant that I could never be certain it was going to happen. British production has no continuity. Each project has its own financial structure, its own chequebook, whatever the past credits of the filmmakers. The producers, Marc and Peter Samuelson, and the director, Brian Gilbert, had made *Tom and Viv*, a film that was well received and profitable, but *Wilde* had to be put together from scratch. The perceived disappointment (financial disappointment, that is) of the film of Christopher Hampton's play *Total Eclipse*, with Leonardo di Caprio as Rimbaud and David Thewlis as Verlaine, led me to believe, doomily, that the equation 'literary faggots = box-office poison' was being chalked up on all Hollywood blackboards.

Without American money or promises of American distribution, our film would founder, and this was not the kind of film into which an American star could be even halfway convincingly sandwiched. I remember saying to Jeremy Irons at some industry wingding last year that I would believe I was truly cast, and not about to be replaced by a big name, only when a production car arrived to pick me up at my home and take me to the set for the first day's shooting. 'No,' Irons said. 'When the car *returns you home* from the first day. That's when you know.' When the cameras finally did roll, then, it came as something more than a relief to wave farewell to the wretched world of preparation and to the imprisonment of endless choice. Filming is, at bottom, blessedly technical. It's about hitting marks, staying in frame, fighting light and learning lines.

What is preparation, after all? Preparation and research are hot buttons hit by all interviewers when talking to film actors. 'What research did you do?' 'How did you prepare?' So far as I can tell, they don't ask concert pianists the same questions, but then concert pianists can't offer good copy along the lines of 'I put on forty pounds in two weeks', or 'I became a voluntary inmate in an asylum for the criminally insane', or 'I lived among Kurdish rebels for ten years', or 'I cut my head off and learned to talk by pulsing my navel in Morse code.'

How did I prepare to play Oscar? The answer is that I really do not know. Acting, especially film acting, is simultaneously mysterious and banal. This is neither to raise it above nor to lower it beneath any other form of endeavour, for the same qualities, I suspect, hold true in tailoring, dentistry and claims adjusting. Unfortunately, an emphasis on the mystery of acting sounds like hideously unacceptable pretension, and an emphasis on its banality sounds like disingenuous philistinism. The mediahedin's appetite for film information grows on what it feeds on. No one outside the worlds of engineering, carpentry or insurance wants to understand their processes, but everyone, it seems, wants to be able to talk about magic hour, aspect ratios, Foley edits, jibbing, crabbing, panning and actors' choices, whatever the hell they are.

Furthermore, any film of a more than minuscule budget these days comes with its own Electronic Press Kit, or EPK – one of those featurettes about the making of a movie. Before a film is out, we've all seen the storyboard, read the screenplay, marvelled at the SFX computer arrays in Seattle, and lived through the production crises with the producer, the director and the actors. The unkind have suggested that some EPKs, such as *The Making of Independence Day*, offer a much more stimulating and coherent narrative than their parent movies. The real advantage for all, however, is that the interviews and the shootings of shootings which the EPK contains can be controlled and efficiently channelled through to the numberless *Entertainment Tonight*-style programmes that now litter the floor of global TV like used lottery scratch cards, which allows the big names to do a great deal of their interviewing in one hit, freeing them up to spend more time with their ranch managers and divorce attorneys. Most of them have no choice in the matter. It's all there in the contract, next to the moral-turpitude rider and the agreement to undergo spot urine tests for Class A drugs, but when explanation crashes through the front door, mystery creeps blushing out the back.

The irony – or the joke, perhaps – about making a film on Wilde is that the process described above is a refinement on Wilde's own celebrity of a hundred years ago: a created thing that might be offered as a boilerplate for all the celebrity mania that was to follow. Wilde was nationally famous before he had written a single memorable work – famous as an undergraduate, famous for being famous, and pilloried in the cartoons and comic cuts for his exotic dress sense and his too utterly-utter aesthetic sensibilities. He was paid to tour the United States to publicize *Patience*, a Gilbert and Sullivan operetta that guyed him and his circle. Certainly he earned his fame later, with the huge success and notoriety of his literary and dramatic works. But up until his trial, in 1893, the public view of Wilde was that the most famous thing about him was his fame – a logic loop all too familiar to contemporary celebrities.

*

I can remember the first time I heard of Beatrix Potter. I can remember the first time I heard of Harriet Beecher Stowe. I can recall with piercing clarity the moment when the name Fyodor Dostoyevsky first came to my ears. (It was in a Norwich café bearing the improbable name Just John's Delicatique.) No matter how hard I try, however, I am unable to think of a time before I had heard of Oscar Wilde. It is as if he had been with me always, like Christ and the Queen.

Not just with me, either. I have tried this out with god-children and nephews of the tenderest years and the most Disneyfied sensibilities. Just as offering 'Scooby what?' will result in an immediate 'Doo', so asking 'Oscar what?' will produce an instant 'Wilde'. In our vulgar world, the name Oscar Wilde has become a logo. And the name has an existence quite independent of the life of Oscar Fingal O'Flahertie Wills Wilde, born 1854, died 1900 – a man none of us has ever met. The name has a meaning wholly distinct, too, from the works of Oscar Wilde: plays, poems, criticism, articles, essays, short stories, children's tales and a novel.

And what of Wilde the man? He stood for Art. He stood for nothing less all his life. His doctrine of Art was so high that most people thought he was joking. The English, who to this day believe themselves quite mistakenly to be pos-sessed of a higher sense of humour than any other nation on earth, have never understood that a thing expressed with wit is more, not less, likely to be true than a thing intoned gravely as solemn fact. We British, who pride our-selves on our superior sense of irony, have never fully grasped the idea of fiction – of *ironism*. Plain old sarcasm is about our mark. When Wilde made an epigram, it was, at best, 'clever'. Clever, like funny, is an English insult of the deepest kind. That minority of English men and women who rejoiced in Wilde's downfall because they were truly sickened by the idea of one man's carnal association with another are almost to be admired, for there was at least a kind of honesty in their hysteria. Most of the hands that were rubbed in glee when Wilde fell were rubbed because all that he stood for fell with him. Damn Wilde for the dull and uninteresting crime of putting his organ of generation in certain places and there was no need to contemplate his real crime, which was not sexual inversion but moral, political, spiritual and artistic inversion. His imprisonment allowed late Victorian England to roll up into a sack the work he had done and hurl it like a poxed odalisque into the Bosphorus. In that sense, the public exposure of his homosexuality was a great intellectual disaster: it contaminated the greatness of his work in the eyes of the world, most especially his work in discursive prose.

A hundred years later, it is Victorian life that is disgraced in our eyes, and Wilde stands now as the Crown Prince of Bohemia: an almost messianic figure to those who want to show their allegiance to Art and Beauty; a saint to those whose recently legitimated sexuality needs its heroes and martyrs; a role model to those who in adolescence have glimpsed the possibilities of self-realization and now tremble terrified on the brink of bourgeoisification. To call Wilde messianic sounds overblown and risks nasty letters from the religious, but there are obvious parallels with the life of Christ. Wilde was despised and rejected; he made fools of the pharisaical elements of society; he had disciples; he was betrayed by one he loved; he sat in his red plush Chelsea Gethsemane knocking back the hock and seltzer while all those around him told him to flee before the entrance of the soldiers, a scene that was neatly retold by John Betjeman:

> 'Mr Woilde we 'ave come for tew take yew
> Where felons and criminals dwell
> We must ask yew tew leave with us quoietly
> For this *is* the Cadogan Hotel.'

Then he rose again to become within a short time after his death the most widely read and translated English-language author in Europe after Shakespeare, and he lives with us now in boxer shorts, playing cards, coffee mugs, coasters and pencil sharpeners.

In our age – which mistakes, as did Wilde's, style for culture and culture for art – is Oscar now just a symbol, however potent? Besides, how dare one assume that the case for Wilde is proved? Despite his hyperbolic image, there are millions out there who have only the dimmest sense of him.

A gentleman approached me one day when we were shooting *Wilde* in Hyde Park. 'What's all this, then?' he wanted to know.

'We're making a film about the life of Oscar Wilde,' I replied.

'Ah, the great man himself,' the gentleman said, nodding wisely. 'I have a record of him singing live, you know.'

'Excuse me?'

'Yes, live at the Desert Inn, Las Vegas. The best version of "Mad Dogs and Englishmen" you'll ever hear.'

I have said that there was never a time I could remember when I had not heard of Wilde. I had great need of him. Without trampling once more over the well-trodden ground of English public school education, I must ask you to picture me at the age of thirteen, on a rugby field deep in the heart of the English countryside, shivering, scared and miserable. Waterloo may have been won on the playing fields, but it was not the only battle to be fought there. I drew up lines between the athletic and the aesthetic, the barbaric and the beautiful, the prose and the passion, the inner and outer lives of *Howard's End*. 'Only connect' was not my text, however. This was war. Early knowledge of my homosexuality only served to define the issue more clearly. There was a world of brutish shouts, mud, tribal intolerance, boasting about girls and contempt for ideas, and there was another world, whose doorway stood in the school library.

God knows how many books I found there to endorse my tiresomely traditional solipsistic achings – biography, autobiography and slim volume after slim volume cataloguing the pansy path to freedom. From Norman Douglas to Robin Maugham, by way of Gide and Peyrefitte, I read – jasper cigarette holder in hand and tasselled smoking cap on head – how the dark clouds of post-Victorian philistinism could give way to the Mediterranean sunlight in Florence, Capri or North Africa. Beckford and Byron had travelled the same route a century earlier, but it was Wilde whose spirit reigned at these feasts of light and colour and silks and poetry and carnal freedom.

That last point sticks, of course. Are we talking sexual

tourism here? Is this what all that high talk comes down to – a greasy intellectual and pseudo-aesthetic justification for following the pervert's pilgrim trail to Tangier? Well, hypocrisy is never good, and I cannot deny that, as a flushed adolescent in a dusty library, much of the thrill I got from reading of the world of the aesthete came from the notion of a place where one could swan about in costly raiment with houseboys and ephebes in tow – and not a rugby player in sight.

Thank the Lord I was born too late for all that, for the sun has set on that world, and I can utter a pretty convinced good riddance to it. There was never anything greatly ennobling in the theory of it, and, frankly, the practice, for all its camp refinements, never endowed the practitioner with any more artistic glamour or literary credibility than calling a rent boy up to a hotel room does today.

Yet, even in my relatively recent adolescence, Wilde – except for *The Importance of Being Earnest*, which through the genius of its perfection was separated from the personality of its author and granted a kind of amnesty – stood only for the unspeakable vice, for secrecy, shame and exposure. John Lehmann, who was a contemporary of Harold Acton, Cyril Connolly and Brian Howard at Eton in the twenties, recalled in his autobiography the day when the headmaster, Cyril Alington, 'a man who delighted in intellectual surprises and paradox', took as the text for his chapel sermon Wilde's *The Happy Prince*.

When the name of the prisoner of Reading Gaol boomed forth in those hallowed surroundings one could immediately sense the change in the atmosphere. Scarcely any boy dared to look at the opposite pews except in a glazed rigid way; jaws were clenched and blushes mounted involuntarily to innumerable cheeks. It was a moment of horror and panic: no one knew what was coming next, and everyone was thinking exactly the same thing.

Any gay man will recall the adolescent experience of watching television with his parents and flushing fiercely when a word like 'homosexual' was used or when a gay pride march was featured on the news. The name Wilde, even fifty years after Lehmann's schooldays, still sent fire to my cheeks when it was publicly spoken, for all the fire he may have lent my spirit when privately contemplated.

I admire, therefore – I truly admire – those heterosexual insiders who set a high value on Wilde. There is a purity in their motive. It was easy enough for a Jewish nancy boy like me to draw solace from Wilde the outcast, Wilde the sexual renegade, Wilde the Irishman, Wilde the mocker and baiter of the imperial values that still hung in the air above the parade ground like Crimean cannon smoke. Had I, by the tiniest genetic alteration, been good at rugby and stirred by girls, would I then have been able to see the real point of Wilde? Or would I, like so many of my country-men, have thought of him (if at all) as not much more than a brittle, queeny wag with crimped hair, a possible source of inspiration when trawling the dictionary of quotations for a best man's speech, but of no more meaning and no more importance? Well, we have to start somewhere, and if nothing else will lead us towards truth the loins may as well. Just as long as the heart and the mind follow and finally overtake, then maybe nothing has been lost. Perhaps there is nothing so very bad after all in finding reality by following an illusion: there is at least gold at the end of Wilde's rainbow. To chase Judy Garland as a gay alternative to beastly real life may be warm and sweet and cosy, but there is nothing over her rainbow but the black-and-white reality of the familial back yard. The Munchkins don't exist; it was all a dream.

I was about seventeen when I emerged from my Firbank, Douglas, Acton and Howard phases. I don't regret my teenage posturings and the fantasy years of collecting limp leather editions of decadent, consumptive poets and penning violet-inked diary entries, but these days I must confess that, if pushed, I would rather lose every Oriental silk dressing gown I own than a single pair of sensible corduroy trousers. *Autres temps, autres pantalons.*

I still retain affection for that luxuriantly poisonous style, but it is, I suppose, not much more than literary drag, and, like so many drag acts, it can become tiresome. At any rate, it has nothing whatever to do with Oscar Wilde or his works. Indeed, such images are only part of what the current jargon labels the 'self-oppression' to which we are all prey. Wilde's courage lay not in his 'alternative sexuality' but in the freedom of his mind. To picture him primarily as a gay martyr *avant la lettre* is, I think, to play into the very hands of those who brought him down a hundred years ago.

*

Yet I know that it is the sexuality and, most especially, the sex that will excite the interest of the press – above all the British press – when *Wilde* is released. I have had advance notice. A few months ago, the Sunday edition of the *Daily*

Mail published a piece on Jude Law, the astonishingly talented young actor in *Wilde* who plays Lord Alfred Douglas, Wilde's lover, the beautiful, petulant and tempestuous youth known as Bosie. (It was Wilde's relationship with Bosie, the son of the Marquess of Queensberry, that brought him to trial and subsequent imprisonment.) The *Mail* decided that there was a story in the fact that I am gay and Jude is straight, and so it reported that during our 'love scenes' together I had to have my penis taped to my stomach to spare my own blushes, not to mention those of Jude Law and the crew. I stared at this story (apparently given to the *Mail* by an insider on the set) amused and amazed, quite undecided as to whether to be flattered or insulted. The fact is that I never actually had to take all my clothes off during the shooting of the film. Wilde, it is generally agreed, did not like to have Bosie Douglas see him naked, for Bosie was not much aroused by Oscar's generous helpings of flesh. So the story was entirely, wholly untrue. For the *Mail*, however, it was a story too good to check. The newspaper wanted it to be true: it had to be true, for it reduced Wilde and his nature (and me and mine, not that that matters much) to the level of sexual beast. Fry is a whoopsy. He had to lie next to an attractive young man, therefore he must have sustained an ungovernable erection. It stands, as it were, to reason. 'The penis mightier than the word' has long been the slogan of the British newspaper editor.

'In the old days men had the rack. Now they have the Press.' So Wilde wrote in *The Soul of Man Under Socialism*. 'In France they manage these things better ... They limit the journalist, and allow the artist almost perfect freedom. Here we allow absolute freedom to the journalist, and entirely limit the artist. English public opinion, that is to say, tries to constrain and impede and warp the man who makes things that are beautiful in effect, and compels the journalist to retail things that are ugly, or disgusting or revolting in fact, so that we have the most serious journalists in the world and the most indecent newspapers.' Wilde was very forgiving, however, and he went on to say of journalists that it was not their fault that they were obliged 'to supply the public with what the public wants ... It is a very degrading position for any body of educated men to be placed in, and I have no doubt that most of them feel it acutely.'

Wilde's forgiveness makes me ashamed of my own intolerance of and anger towards the ghastliness of tabloid journalism. I would like to hope that playing Wilde taught me the humility to be arrogant enough to empathize. It certainly confronted me with endless examples of that primary paradox of his greatness. Wilde's life was one of supreme individualism, but its effect was one of supreme generosity. To fulfil his real self – the eternal Socratic goal – he followed through in life the artistic technique of the imaginative penetration of the lives of others.

When his friend Oswald Sickert died, Wilde went to Sickert's home to comfort his bereaved wife, but was told that she was inconsolable and seeing no one. He persisted till the widow finally agreed to see him, and talked to her hour after hour about her husband, conjuring him back to life with memories and anecdote. Her wailing turned to laughter. Remarkably enough, Wilde even charmed the Marquess of Queensberry on their first meeting. Bosie and

Wilde had been lunching *à deux* at the Café Royal when Queensberry came into the room. Bosie approached his father and invited him to Wilde's table. Queensberry reluctantly consented. After twenty minutes, Bosie left them together, deep in conversation, where they remained for the rest of the afternoon.

*

Oddly, therefore, the chief memory I have of playing Oscar is not one of spouting epigrams and setting the table in a roar but one of listening and reacting. W. B. Yeats remarked what a great listener Wilde was, and Sir Arthur Conan Doyle is said to have once left a dinner party raving about the man's gift as a conversationalist. 'But you did all the talking,' his companion pointed out. 'Exactly!' Conan Doyle said. To follow Wilde's life on film – often to be actually saying the very things he said in the very places he said them, in the Café Royal in Piccadilly, or walking along the same path he and Bosie Douglas walked along when they first got to know each other, in the gardens of Magdalen College, Oxford – is a disorienting experience. I couldn't possibly be Wilde, but, at further risk of pretension, I certainly feel that playing him has somehow allowed me to be more myself.

I am often asked what I think Wilde would make of our film. All I can be certain of is that he would be kind about it. When Wilde hit upon the idea of Dorian Gray, the beautiful youth who stays young while his portrait ages and takes on the scars of his dissipation, he kept quiet about it. He had once revealed another story idea at the dinner table only to find it written up in a magazine a month later.

He wrote to the plagiarist to say that stealing the story was the act of a gentleman, but neglecting to tell Wilde that he had stolen it was not. Such affable chiding was as bitchy as Wilde got. Most people remember the story of Wilde's saying, in response to a witticism, 'I wish I had said that,' and Whistler's famous reply, 'You will, Oscar, you will.' That exchange tells us everything we need to know about the difference between Whistler and Wilde.

*

De Profundis, the letter that Wilde wrote to Bosie Douglas from prison, is, so far as I know, the greatest and most honest letter ever written. Its title means 'from the depths', and it sets out in painfully beautiful language the history of Wilde's relationship with Bosie, his sense of how his life went wrong, and his interpretation of what prison and suffering had taught him. 'The supreme vice is shallowness. Whatever is realized is right' was Wilde's last great chime, and he struck it again and again in *De Profundis*. To discover the self and develop it to its full realization, that is our duty, Wilde wrote. He knew perfectly well that his downfall would be perceived as the downfall of this philosophy:

People point to Reading Gaol, and say 'That is where the artistic life leads a man.' Well, it might lead to worse places. The more mechanical people ... always know where they are going, and go there ... A man whose desire is to be something separate from himself, to be a Member of Parliament, or a successful grocer, or a prominent solicitor, or a judge, or something equally tedious, invariably succeeds in being what he wants to be.

That is his punishment. Those who want a mask have to wear

it. But with the dynamic forces of life ... it is different. People whose desire is solely for self-realization never know where they are going. They can't know.

This is the sticking point for many. To hear what they think of as their reward in life being described as a punishment infuriates them, and it could infuriate them only because they suspect it to be true. This is why Wilde is still the Crown Prince of Bohemia. We stand at a threshold in our lives where we look into our futures and see the permanent attachment of a mask, the final adoption of a set of values and 'core beliefs' which will see us through to the end, and then we turn and look back at the gigantic, Promethean figure of Wilde – whether we picture him, cigarette in hand, at a table in the Café Royal, generous in wit and high on fame, or bowed over a deal table in a prison cell and cramped with dysentery – and ask ourselves if we have the courage to be like him, by which we mean the courage to be like ourselves.

*

Whether *Wilde* the movie will 'take' or not I cannot possibly guess. Some may be furious over sins of omission or commission; others may baulk at its candor or necessary compression of detail. I know there will be letters telling me 'When Wilde was arrested, Reggie Turner was in the room, yet you have him alone with Robbie Ross', or 'You have him facing the jury in court, but in fact the jury was behind him', and so on.

We come down to this: Wilde was a great writer and a great man. Great in his kindness, great in his sympathy and great in his courage. He is still enormously underestimated as an artist and a thinker, especially in his adopted land of England. The subject of *Wilde* the film is not Oscar Wilde's work but his life, yet if it turns any one person to his writings, and most especially to the essays, to the stories for children and to *De Profundis*, then it will have been of some service. For my part, I should be able to return to playing stock English foils, corrupt lawyers, Persian-cat-stroking villains and epicene fools with a lighter heart.

Stephen Fry

Note on the Text

The aim, as far as possible, has been to print this selection in chronological order of the date of first publication of published works (or production in the case of plays). However, this has presented some difficulties when placing verbal or conversational quotations attributed to Wilde where exact dates are unknown. In such instances quotations have been placed in a thematically appropriate context.

Nothing ... Except My Genius

* * *

If you ask nine-tenths of the British public what is the meaning of the word aesthetics, they will tell you it is the French for affectation or the German for a dado ...

Lecture: *The English Renaissance of Art,* 9 January 1882

To know nothing about their great men is one of the necessary elements of English education.

And criticism – what place is that to have in our culture? Well, I think that the first duty of an art critic is to hold his tongue at all times, and upon all subjects: *C'est une grande avantage de n'avoir rien fait, mais il ne faut pas en abuser.*

Art can never have any other claim but her own perfection: it is for the critic to create for art the social aim, too, by teaching the people the spirit in which they are to approach all artistic work, the love they are to give it, the lesson they are to draw from it.

... beauty is the only thing that time cannot harm. Philosophies fall away like sand, and creeds follow one another like the withered leaves of autumn; but what is beautiful is a joy for all seasons and a possession for all eternity.

... the good we get from art is not what we learn from it; it is what we become through it.

We spend our days, each one of us, in looking for the secret of life. Well, the secret of life is in art.

* * *

Had I been treated differently by the newspapers in England and in this country, had I been commended and endorsed, for the first time in my life I should have doubted myself and my mission ... What possible difference can it make to me what the *New York Herald* says? You go and look at the statue of the Venus de Milo and you know that it is an exquisitely beautiful creation. Would it change your opinion in the least if all the newspapers in the land should pronounce it a wretched caricature? Not at all. I know that I am right, that I have a mission to perform. I am indestructible!

Letter to *Rochester Democrat and Chronicle*, 8 February 1882

* * *

The supreme object of life is to live. Few people live. It is true life only to realize one's own perfection, to make one's every dream a reality.

Interview in *Omaha Weekly Herald*, 24 March 1882

* * *

To me the life of the businessman who eats his breakfast early in the morning, catches a train for the city, stays there in the dingy, dusty atmosphere of the commercial world, and goes back to his house in the evening, and after supper to sleep, is worse than the life of the galley slave – his chains are golden instead of iron.

Interview in *Topeka Capital*, April 1882

* * *

* * *

Bad art is a great deal worse than no art at all.
> Lecture: *The Practical Application of the Principles of*
> *Aesthetic Theory to Exterior and Interior House Decoration,*
> *with Observations upon Dress and Personal Ornaments,*
> 11 May 1882

No better way is there to learn to love Nature than to understand Art. It dignifies every flower of the field. And, the boy who sees the thing of beauty which a bird on the wing becomes when transferred to wood or canvas will probably not throw the customary stone. What we want is something spiritual added to life. Nothing is so ignoble that Art cannot sanctify it.

* * *

* * *

I would rather have discovered Mrs [Lillie] Langtry than have discovered America. (Attrib.)

* * *

In the evening I went to the Casino ... There I found the miners and the female friends of the miners, and in one corner a pianist – sitting at a piano over which was this notice: 'Please don't shoot the pianist; he is doing his best.' I was struck with this recognition of the fact that bad art merits the penalty of death, and I felt that in this remote city, where the aesthetic applications of the revolver were clearly established in the case of music, my apostolic task would be much simplified, as indeed it was.

The World, 7 March 1883

* * *

* * *

... nothing is worth doing except what the world says is impossible. *Lecture to Art Students,* 30 June 1883

* * *

Today more than ever the artist and a love of the beautiful are needed to temper and counteract the sordid materialism of the age. In an age when science has undertaken to declaim against the soul and spiritual nature of man, and when commerce is ruining beautiful rivers and magnificent woodlands and the glorious skies in its greed for gain, the artist comes forward as a priest and prophet of nature to protest ... *The House Beautiful*

* * *

* * *

To make a good salad is to be a brilliant diplomatist – the problem is entirely the same in both cases. To know exactly how much oil one must put with one's vinegar.

Vera, or The Nihilists

Life is much too important a thing ever to talk seriously about it.

There is always more brass than brains in an aristocracy.

Good kings are the only dangerous enemies that modern democracy has.

* * *

* * *

I am going to be married to a beautiful girl called Constance Lloyd, a grave, slight, violet-eyed little Artemis,
with great coils of heavy brown hair which make her
flower-like head droop like a blossom, and wonderful
ivory hands which draw music from the piano so sweet
that the birds stop singing to listen to her. We are to be
married in April. I hope so much that you will be over then.
I am so anxious for you to know and to like her.

I am hard at work lecturing and getting rich, though it is
horrid being so much away from her, but we telegraph to
each other twice a day, and I rush back suddenly from the
uttermost parts of the earth to see her for an hour, and do
all the foolish things that wise lovers do.

Letter to Lillie Langtry

* * *

* * *

To My Wife
WITH A COPY OF MY POEMS

I can write no stately proem
 As a prelude to my lay;
From a poet to a poem
 I would dare to say.

For if of these fallen petals
 One to you seem fair,
Love will waft it till it settles
 On your hair.

And when wind and winter harden
 All the loveless land,
It will whisper of the garden
 You will understand.

* * *

* * *

I have always been of the opinion that consistency is the last refuge of the unimaginative ...

Pall Mall Gazette, 28 February 1885

* * *

... the British cook is a foolish woman, who should be turned, for her iniquities, into a pillar of that salt which she never knows how to use.

Pall Mall Gazette, 7 March 1885

* * *

Of Shakespeare it may be said he was the first to see the dramatic value of doublets, and that a climax may depend on a crinoline.   *The Truth of Masks*

... the stage is not merely the meeting-place of all the arts, but is also the return of art to life.

Art has no other aim but her own perfection, and proceeds simply by her own laws ...

The true dramatist ... shows us life under the conditions of art, not art in the form of life.

The facts of art are diverse, but the essence of artistic effect is unity. Monarchy, Anarchy and Republicanism may contend for the government of nations; but a theatre should be in the power of a cultured despot. There may be division of labour, but there must be no division of mind ... In fact, in art there is no specialism, and a really artistic production should bear the impress of one master, and one master only, who not merely should design and arrange everything, but should have complete control over the way in which each dress is to be worn.

*   *   *

... our ordinary English novelists ... fail ... in concentration of style. Their characters are far too eloquent and talk themselves to tatters. What we want is a little more reality and a little less rhetoric ... we wish that they would talk less and think more. They lead us through a barren desert of verbiage to a mirage that they call life: we wander aimlessly through a very wilderness of words in search of one touch of nature. However, one should not be too severe on English novels; they are the only relaxation of the intellectually unemployed.　　*Pall Mall Gazette*, 4 August 1886

* * *

A poet can survive everything but a misprint.
　　　　　　　　Pall Mall Gazette, 14 October 1886

* * *

... a poet without hysterics is rare.
　　　　　　　　Pall Mall Gazette, 8 March 1887

* * *

... English people are far more interested in American barbarism than they are in American civilization.

Court and Society Review, 23 March 1887

In America the young are always ready to give to those who are older than themselves the full benefits of their inexperience ... it may be truly said that no American child is ever blind to the deficiencies of its parents, no matter how much it may love them.

There is no such thing as a stupid American. Many Americans are horrid, vulgar, intrusive and impertinent, just as many English people are also; but stupidity is not one of the national vices. Indeed, in America there is no opening for a fool. They expect brains even from a boot-black, and get them.

As for marriage, it is one of their most popular institutions. The American man marries early, and the American woman marries often; and they get on extremely well together.

On the whole, the great success of marriage in the States is due partly to the fact that no American man is ever idle, and partly to the fact that no American wife is considered responsible for the quality of her husband's dinners.

* * *

America has never quite forgiven Europe for having been discovered somewhat earlier in history than itself.

Court and Society Review, 13 April 1887

* * *

... it would be a very good thing if people were taught how to speak. Language is the noblest instrument we have, either for the revealing or the concealing of thought; talk itself is a sort of spiritualized action; and conversation is one of the loveliest of the arts.

Court and Society Review, 4 May 1887

* * *

The only form of fiction in which real characters do not seem out of place is history.

Saturday Review, 7 May 1887

* * *

Early in life she had discovered the important truth that nothing looks so like innocence as an indiscretion; and by a series of reckless escapades, half of them quite harmless, she had acquired all the privileges of a personality. She had more than once changed her husband; indeed, Debrett credits her with three marriages; but as she had never changed her lover, the world had long ago ceased to talk scandal about her.

'Lord Arthur Savile's Crime', May 1887

* * *

Unless one is wealthy there is no use in being a charming fellow. Romance is the privilege of the rich, not the profession of the unemployed. The poor should be practical and prosaic. It is better to have a permanent income than to be fascinating.   *The Model Millionaire*

We have really everything in common with America nowadays, except, of course, language.

The Canterville Ghost

* * *

Nobody, even in the provinces, should ever be allowed to ask an intelligent question about pure mathematics across a dinner table. A question of this kind is quite as bad as inquiring suddenly about the state of a man's soul ...

Pall Mall Gazette, 16 December 1887

Really domestic people are almost invariably bad talkers, as their very virtues in home life have dulled their interests in outer things. The very best mothers will insist on chattering of their babies, and prattling about infant education. In fact most women do not take sufficient interest in politics, just as most men are deficient in general reading. Still, anybody can be made to talk, except the very obstinate, and even a commercial traveller may be drawn out, and become quite interesting.

* * *

* * *

The health of a nation depends very largely on its mode of dress; the artistic feeling of a nation should find expression in its costume quite as much as in its architecture...

Woman's World, January 1888

* * *

As a general rule, his verse is full of pretty echoes of other writers, but in one sonnet he makes a distinct attempt to be original and the result is extremely depressing.

> Earth wears her grandest robe, by autumn spun,
> *Like some stout matron who of youth has run*
> *The course, ...*

is the most dreadful simile we have ever come across, even in poetry. Mr Griffiths should beware of originality. Like beauty, it is a fatal gift.

Pall Mall Gazette, 15 February 1888

* * *

But what is the good of friendship if one cannot say exactly what one means? Anybody can say charming things and try to please and to flatter, but a true friend always says unpleasant things, and does not mind giving pain. Indeed, if he is a really true friend he prefers it, for he knows that then he is doing good.   *The Devoted Friend*

* * *

... anybody can have common sense, provided that they have no imagination.   *The Remarkable Rocket*

The only thing that sustains one through life is the consciousness of the immense inferiority of everybody else, and this is a feeling that I have always cultivated.

I am so clever that sometimes I don't understand a single word of what I am saying.

I have always been of opinion that hard work is simply the refuge of people who have nothing whatever to do.

* * *

* * *

All that is known by that term [*fin de siècle*] I particularly admire and love. It is the fine flower of our civilization: the only thing that keeps the world from the commonplace, the coarse, the barbarous.   Letter to Leo Maxse

The term *fin de siècle* was associated
with artistic Decadence

* * *

Flaubert did not write French prose, but the prose of a great artist who happened to be French.

Letter to W. E. Henley

* * *

* * *

I was thinking in bed this morning that the great superiority of France over England is that in France every bourgeois wants to be an artist, whereas in England every artist wants to be a bourgeois. (Attrib.)

Prayer must never be answered: if it is, it ceases to be prayer and becomes correspondence. (Attrib.)

I have made an important discovery ... that alcohol, taken in sufficient quantities, produces all the effects of intoxication. (Attrib.)

Missionaries, my dear! Don't you realize that missionaries are the divinely provided food for destitute and underfed cannibals? Whenever they are on the brink of starvation, Heaven in its infinite mercy sends them a nice plump missionary. (Attrib.)

Philosophy teaches us to bear with equanimity the misfortunes of others. (Attrib.)

* * *

* * *

As a rule the model, nowadays, is a pretty girl, from about twelve to twenty-five years of age, who knows nothing about art, cares less and is merely anxious to earn seven or eight shillings a day without much trouble. English models rarely look at a picture, and never venture on any aesthetic theories. In fact they realize very completely Mr Whistler's idea of the function of an art critic, for they pass no criticisms at all.

English Illustrated Magazine, January 1889

* * *

My own experience is that the more we study Art, the less we care for Nature ... Art is our spirited protest, our gallant attempt to teach Nature her proper place.

Vivian in *The Decay of Lying*

Thinking is the most unhealthy thing in the world, and people die of it just as they die of any other disease. Fortunately, in England at any rate, thought is not catching.

Lying and poetry are arts – arts, as Plato saw, not unconnected with each other – and they require the most careful study, the most disinterested devotion.

M. Zola is determined to show that, if he has not got genius, he can at least be dull.

In literature we require distinction, charm, beauty and imaginative power. We don't want to be harrowed and disgusted with an account of the doings of the lower orders.

I quite admit that modern novels have many good points. All I insist on is that, as a class, they are quite unreadable.

George Meredith. His style is chaos illuminated by flashes of lightning. As a writer he has mastered everything except language: as a novelist he can do everything except tell a story: as an artist he is everything except articulate.

Art takes life as part of her rough material, recreates it and refashions it in fresh forms, is absolutely indifferent to fact, invents, imagines, dreams and keeps between herself and reality the impenetrable barrier of beautiful style, of decorative or ideal treatment.

Art itself is really a form of exaggeration; and selection, which is the very spirit of art, is nothing more than an intensified mode of over-emphasis.

The proper school to learn art in is not Life but Art.

Facts are not merely finding a footing-place in history, but they are usurping the domain of Fancy, and have invaded the kingdom of Romance. Their chilling touch is over everything. They are vulgarizing mankind.

Society sooner or later must return to its lost leader, the cultured and fascinating liar.

Literature always anticipates life. It does not copy it, but moulds it to its purpose.

Life imitates Art far more than Art imitates Life ... Life holds the mirror up to Art, and either reproduces some strange type imagined by painter or sculptor, or realizes in fact what has been dreamed in fiction.

For what is Nature? Nature is no great mother who has borne us. She is our creation. It is in our brain that she quickens to life. Things are because we see them, and what we see, and how we see it, depends on the Arts that have influenced us. To look at a thing is very different from seeing a thing. One does not see anything until one sees its beauty. Then, and then only, does it come into existence.

... imitation can be made the sincerest form of insult.

Yesterday evening Mrs Arundel insisted on my going to the window, and looking at the glorious sky, as she called it. Of course I had to look at it. She is one of those absurdly pretty Philistines to whom one can deny nothing. And what was it? It was simply a very second-rate Turner, a Turner of a bad period, with all the painter's worst faults exaggerated and over-emphasized.

The more abstract, the more ideal an art is, the more it reveals to us the temper of its age. If we wish to understand a nation by means of its art, let us look at its architecture or its music.

The fact is that we look back on the ages entirely through the medium of art, and art, very fortunately, has never once told us the truth.

* * *

To become a work of art is the object of living.

(Attrib.)

The English are always degrading truths into facts. When a truth becomes a fact it loses all its intellectual value.

(Attrib.)

* * *

There is a great deal to be said in favour of reading a novel backwards. The last page is as a rule the most interesting, and when one begins with the catastrophe or the *dénouement* one feels on pleasant terms of equality with the author. It is like going behind the scenes of a theatre. One is no longer taken in, and the hair-breadth escapes of the hero and the wild agonies of the heroine leave one absolutely unmoved. One knows the jealously-guarded secret, and one can afford to smile at the quite unnecessary anxiety that the puppets of fiction always consider it their duty to display.　　*Pall Mall Gazette,* 5 June 1889

* * *

* * *

All charming people, I fancy, are spoiled. It is the secret of
their attraction.   Erskine in *The Portrait of Mr W. H.*

It is always a silly thing to give advice, but to give good
advice is absolutely fatal. I hope you will never fall into
that error. If you do, you will be sorry for it.

You forget that a thing is not necessarily true because a
man dies for it.

Art, even the art of fullest scope and widest vision, can
never really show us the external world. All that it shows
us is our own soul, the one world of which we have any real
cognizance ... It is Art, and Art only, that reveals us to
ourselves.

* * *

* * *

A critic should be taught to criticize a work of art without making any reference to the personality of the author. This, in fact, is the beginning of criticism.

Letter to St James's Gazette, 28 June 1890

* * *

... the public is wonderfully tolerant. It forgives everything except genius. Gilbert in *The Critic as Artist*

Every great man nowadays has his disciples, and it is always Judas who writes the biography.

Gilbert: Ernest, you are quite delightful, but your views are terribly unsound. I am afraid that you have been listening to the conversation of some one older than yourself. That is always a dangerous thing to do, and if you allow it to degenerate into a habit you will find it absolutely fatal to any intellectual development. As for modern journalism, it is not my business to defend it. It justifies its own existence by the great Darwinian principle of the survival of the vulgarest. I have merely to do with literature.

Ernest: But what is the difference between literature and journalism?

Gilbert: Oh! journalism is unreadable, and literature is not read. That is all.

Learned conversation is either the affectation of the ignorant or the profession of the mentally unemployed.

Education is an admirable thing. But it is well to remember from time to time that nothing that is worth knowing can be taught.

Without the critical faculty, there is no artistic creation at all worthy of the name.

Anybody can write a three-volume novel. It merely requires a complete ignorance of both life and literature.

Anybody can make history. Only a great man can write it.

Self-denial is simply a method by which man arrests his progress, and self-sacrifice a survival of the mutilation of the savage ...

The world is made by the singer for the dreamer.

The best that one can say of most modern creative art is that it is just a little less vulgar than reality ...

It is sometimes said that the tragedy of an artist's life is that he cannot realize his ideal. But the true tragedy that dogs the steps of most artists is that they realize their ideal too absolutely. For, when the ideal is realized, it is robbed of its wonder and its mystery, and becomes simply a new starting-point for an ideal that is other than itself. This is the reason why music is the perfect type of art.

Conversation should touch everything, but should concentrate itself on nothing.

... life is terribly deficient in form. Its catastrophes happen in the wrong way and to the wrong people. There is a grotesque horror about its comedies, and its tragedies seem to culminate in farce. One is always wounded when one approaches it. Things last either too long or not long enough.

Gilbert: ... Life! Don't let us go to life for our fulfilment or our experience. It is a thing narrowed by circumstances, incoherent in its utterance, and without that fine correspondence of form and spirit which is the only thing that can satisfy the artistic and critical temperament. It makes us pay too high a price for its wares, and we purchase the meanest of its secrets at a cost that is monstrous and infinite.

Ernest: Must we go, then, to Art for everything?

Gilbert: For everything. Because Art does not hurt us. The tears that we shed at a play are a type of the exquisite sterile emotions that it is the function of Art to awaken. We weep, but we are not wounded. We grieve, but our grief is not bitter ... It is through Art, and through Art only, that we can realize our perfection; through Art, and through Art only, that we can shield ourselves from the sordid perils of actual existence.

... to do nothing at all is the most difficult thing in the world, the most difficult and the most intellectual.

... all the arts are immoral, except those baser forms of sensual or didactic art that seek to excite to action of evil or of good. For action of every kind belongs to the sphere of ethics. The aim of art is simply to create a mood.

There is no country in the world so much in need of unpractical people as this country of ours. With us, Thought is degraded by its constant association with practice. We live in the age of the overworked, and the under-educated; the age in which people are so industrious that they become absolutely stupid ...

The sure way of knowing nothing about life is to try to make oneself useful.

... the development of the race depends on the development of the individual, and where self-culture has ceased to be the ideal, the intellectual standard is instantly lowered, and, often, ultimately lost.

It is so easy for people to have sympathy with suffering. It is so difficult for them to have sympathy with thought.

An idea that is not dangerous is unworthy of being called an idea at all.

Man is least himself when he talks in his own person. Give him a mask, and he will tell you the truth.

For what is Truth? In matters of religion, it is simply the opinion that has survived. In matters of science, it is the ultimate sensation. In matters of art, it is one's last mood.

There are two ways of disliking art ... One is to dislike it. The other, to like it rationally.

A little sincerity is a dangerous thing, and a great deal of it is absolutely fatal.

... there is much to be said in favour of modern journalism. By giving us the opinions of the uneducated, it keeps us in touch with the ignorance of the community.

It is only by the cultivation of the habit of intellectual criticism that we shall be able to rise superior to race-prejudices ... Criticism will annihilate race-prejudices, by insisting upon the unity of the human mind in the variety of its forms.

Aesthetics are higher than ethics. They belong to a more spiritual sphere. To discern the beauty of a thing is the finest point to which we can arrive. Even a colour-sense is more important, in the development of the individual, than a sense of right or wrong. Aesthetics, in fact, are to Ethics in the sphere of conscious civilization, what, in the sphere of the external world, sexual is to natural selection. Ethics, like natural selection, make existence possible. Aesthetics, like sexual selection, make life lovely and wonderful, fill it with new forms, and give it progress, and variety and change.

Gilbert: Yes: I am a dreamer. For a dreamer is one who can only find his way by moonlight, and his punishment is that he sees the dawn before the rest of the the world.
  Ernest: His punishment?
  Gilbert: And his reward.

* * *

* * *

The artist is the creator of beautiful things.

To reveal art and conceal the artist is art's aim.

The critic is he who can translate into another manner or a new material his impression of beautiful things.

The highest, as the lowest, form of criticism is a mode of autobiography.

Those who find ugly meanings in beautiful things are corrupt without being charming. This is a fault.

Those who find beautiful meanings in beautiful things are the cultivated. For these there is hope.

They are the elect to whom beautiful things mean only Beauty.

There is no such thing as a moral or an immoral book. Books are well written, or badly written. That is all.

The nineteenth-century dislike of Realism is the rage of Caliban seeing his own face in the glass.

The nineteenth-century dislike of Romanticism is the rage of Caliban not seeing his own face in a glass.

The moral life of man forms part of the subject-matter of the artist, but the morality of art consists in the perfect use of an imperfect medium. No artist desires to prove anything. Even things that are true can be proved.

No artist has ethical sympathies. An ethical sympathy in an artist is an unpardonable mannerism of style.

No artist is ever morbid. The artist can express everything.

Thought and language are to the artist instruments of an art.

Vice and virtue are to the artist materials for an art.

From the point of view of form, the type of all the arts is the art of the musician. From the point of view of feeling, the actor's craft is the type.

All art is at once surface and symbol.

Those who go beneath the surface do so at their peril.

Those who read the symbol do so at their peril.

It is the spectator, and not life, that art really mirrors.

Diversity of opinion about a work of art shows that the work is new, complex and vital.

When critics disagree the artist is in accord with himself.

We can forgive a man for making a useful thing as long as he does not admire it. The only excuse for making a useless thing is that one admires it intensely.

All art is quite useless.

The Preface to *The Picture of Dorian Gray*

Lord Henry: . . . there is only one thing in the world worse than being talked about, and that is not being talked about.

The Picture of Dorian Gray

Lord Henry: . . .the one charm of marriage is that it makes a life of deception absolutely necessary for both parties.

Basil Hallward: . . . every portrait that is painted with feeling is a portrait of the artist, not of the sitter. The sitter is merely the accident, the occasion. It is not he who is revealed by the painter; it is rather the painter who, on the coloured canvas, reveals himself.

Lord Henry: . . . If one puts forward an idea to a true Englishman – always a rash thing to do – he never dreams of considering whether the idea is right or wrong. The only thing he considers of any importance is whether one believes it oneself. Now, the value of an idea has nothing whatsoever to do with the sincerity of the man who expresses it. Indeed, the probabilities are that the more insincere the man is, the more purely intellectual will the idea be, as in that case it will not be coloured by either his wants, his desires, or his prejudices.

Lord Henry: I like persons better than principles, and I like persons with no principles better than anything else in the world.

Lord Henry: The thoroughly well-informed man – that is the modern ideal. And the mind of the thoroughly well-informed man is a dreadful thing. It is like a bric-à-brac shop, all monsters and dust, with everything priced above its proper value.

Lord Henry: And Beauty is a form of Genius – is higher, indeed, than Genius, as it needs no explanation.

'They say that when good Americans die they go to Paris,' chuckled Sir Thomas . . .
    'Really! And where do bad Americans go to when they die?' inquired the Duchess.
    'They go to America,' murmured Lord Henry.

Lord Henry: Humanity takes itself too seriously. It is the world's original sin. If the caveman had known how to laugh, History would have been different.

Lord Henry: Nowadays most people die of a sort of creeping common sense, and discover when it is too late that the only things one never regrets are one's mistakes.

Lady Henry: I like Wagner's music better than anybody's. It is so loud that one can talk the whole time without other people hearing what one says.

Dorian Gray: If one hears bad music, it is one's duty to drown it in conversation.

Lord Henry: Women are a decorative sex. They never have anything to say, but they say it charmingly.

Lord Henry: ... the people who love only once in their lives are really the shallow people. What they call their loyalty, and their fidelity, I call either the lethargy of custom or their lack of imagination. Faithfulness is to the emotional life what consistency is to the life of the intellect – simply a confession of failure.

Lord Henry: When one is in love, one always begins by deceiving one's self, and one always ends by deceiving others. That is what the world calls a romance.

Lord Henry: The only artists I have ever known, who are personally delightful, are bad artists. Good artists exist simply in what they make, and consequently are perfectly uninteresting in what they are.

Experience was of no ethical value. It was merely the name men gave to their mistakes.

Women defend themselves by attacking, just as they attack by sudden and strange surrenders.

Lord Henry: The real drawback to marriage is that it makes one unselfish. And unselfish people are colourless. They lack individuality.

Lord Henry: . . . every experience is of value, and, whatever one may say against marriage, it is certainly an experience.

Lord Henry: The reason we all like to think so well of others is that we are all afraid for ourselves. The basis of optimism is sheer terror. We think that we are generous because we credit our neighbour with the possession of those virtues that are likely to be a benefit to us.

Lord Henry: It is not good for one's morals to see bad acting.

Lord Henry: There are only two kinds of people who are really fascinating – people who know absolutely everything, and people who know absolutely nothing.

There is always something ridiculous about the emotions of people whom one has ceased to love.

There is a luxury in self-reproach. When we blame ourselves we feel that no one else has a right to blame us. It is the confession, not the priest, that gives us absolution.

Lord Henry: ... the only way a woman can ever reform a man is by boring him so completely that he loses all possible interest in life.

Lord Henry: One can always be kind to people about whom one cares nothing.

Lord Henry: Never trust a woman who wears mauve, whatever her age may be, or a woman over thirty-five who is fond of pink ribbons. It always means that they have a history.

Lord Henry: ... nothing makes one so vain as being told one is a sinner.

Is insincerity such a terrible thing? I think not. It is merely a method by which we can multiply our personalities.

Dorian Gray: I know how people chatter in England. The middle classes air their moral prejudices over their gross dinner-tables, and whisper about what they call the profligacies of their betters in order to try and pretend that they are in smart society, and on intimate terms with the people they slander.

Lord Henry: When a woman marries again it is because she detested her first husband. When a man marries again, it is because he adored his first wife. Women try their luck; men risk theirs.

Lord Henry: A man can be happy with any woman as long as he does not love her.

Lord Henry: It is a sad truth, but we have lost the faculty of giving lovely names to things. Names are everything. I never quarrel with actions. My one quarrel is with words. That is the reason I hate vulgar realism in literature. The man who could call a spade a spade should be compelled to use one. It is the only thing he is fit for.

Lord Henry: Romance lives by repetition, and repetition converts an appetite into an art. Besides, each time that one loves is the only time one has ever loved. Difference of object does not alter singleness of passion. It merely intensifies it. We can have in life but one great experience at best, and the secret of life is to reproduce that experience as often as possible.

Shallow sorrows and shallow loves live on. The loves and sorrows that are great are destroyed by their own plenitude.

Lord Henry: . . . anybody can be good in the country. There are no temptations there. That is the reason why people who live out of town are so absolutely uncivilized. Civilization is not by any means an easy thing to attain to. There are only two ways by which man can reach it. One is by being cultured, the other by being corrupt. Country people have no opportunity of being either, so they stagnate.

Lord Henry: Death and vulgarity are the only two facts in the nineteenth century that one cannot explain away.

Lord Henry: All crime is vulgar, just as all vulgarity is crime.

* * *

The critic has to educate the public; the artist has to educate the critic.

> Letter to the *Scots Observer*, 13 August 1890,
> in defence of *The Picture of Dorian Gray*

* * *

* * *

With the abolition of private property, then, we shall have true, beautiful, healthy Individualism. Nobody will waste his life in accumulating things, and the symbols for things. One will live. To live is the rarest thing in the world. Most people exist, that is all.   *The Soul of Man under Socialism*

There is only one class in the community that thinks more about money than the rich, and that is the poor. The poor can think of nothing else. That is the misery of being poor.

High hopes were once formed of democracy; but democracy means simply the bludgeoning of the people by the people for the people.

The fact is, that civilization requires slaves. The Greeks were quite right there. Unless there are slaves to do the ugly, horrible, uninteresting work, culture and contemplation become almost impossible. Human slavery is wrong, insecure and demoralizing. On mechanical slavery, on the slavery of the machine, the future of the world depends.

A work of art is the unique result of a unique temperament ... the moment that an artist takes notice of what other people want, and tries to supply the demand, he ceases to be an artist, and becomes a dull or an amusing craftsman, an honest or a dishonest tradesman.

Now Art should never try to be popular. The public should try to make itself artistic.

In England, the arts that have escaped best are the arts in which the public take no interest. Poetry is an instance of what I mean. We have been able to have fine poetry in England because the public do not read it, and consequently do not influence it.

... the public make use of the classics of a country as a means of checking the progress of Art. They degrade the classics into authorities. They use them as bludgeons for preventing the free expression of Beauty in new forms. They are always asking a writer why he does not write like somebody else, or a painter why he does not paint like somebody else, quite oblivious of the fact that if either of them did anything of the kind he would cease to be an artist.

In the old days men had the rack. Now they have the Press.

In England, Journalism, except in a few well-known instances, not having been carried to such excesses of brutality, is still a great factor, a really remarkable power. The tyranny that it proposes to exercise over people's private lives seems to me to be quite extraordinary. The fact is that the public have an insatiable curiosity to know everything, except what is worth knowing. Journalism, conscious of this, and having tradesman-like habits, supplies their demands. In centuries before ours the public nailed the ears of journalists to the pump. That was quite hideous. In this century journalists have nailed their own ears to the keyhole. That is much worse.

People sometimes inquire what form of government is most suitable for an artist to live under. To this question there is only one answer. The form of government that is most suitable to the artist is no government at all.

Anybody can sympathize with the sufferings of a friend, but it requires a very fine nature – it requires, in fact, that nature of a true Individualist – to sympathize with a friend's success.

* * *

Work is the curse of the drinking classes of this country.

(Attrib.)

* * *

Lord Darlington: I can resist everything except temptation.

Lady Windermere's Fan

Duchess of Berwick: Men become old, but they never become good.

Lady Plymdale: It's most dangerous nowadays for a husband to pay any attention to his wife in public. It always makes people think that he beats her when they're alone. The world has grown so suspicious of anything that looks like a happy married life.

Lady Windermere: London is full of women who trust their husbands. One can always recognize them. They look so thoroughly unhappy.

Lord Darlington: Between men and women there is no friendship possible. There is passion, enmity, worship, love, but no friendship.

Cecil Graham: ... nothing looks so like innocence as an indiscretion.

Cecil Graham: Wicked women bother one. Good women bore one. That is the only difference between them.

Cecil Graham: History is merely gossip. But scandal is gossip made tedious by morality. Now, I never moralize. A man who moralizes is usually a hypocrite, and a woman who moralizes is invariably plain.

Cecil Graham: That is the worst of women. They always want one to be good. And if we are good, when they meet us, they don't love us at all. They like to find us quite irretrievably bad, and to leave us quite unattractively good.

Cecil Graham: ... what on earth should we men do going about with purity and innocence? A carefully thought-out buttonhole is much more effective.

Cecil Graham: What is a cynic?

Lord Darlington: A man who knows the price of everything and the value of nothing.

Cecil Graham: And a sentimentalist, my dear Darlington, is a man who sees an absurd value in everything, and doesn't know the market price of any single thing.

* * *

... the personality of the actor is often a source of danger in the perfect presentation of a work of art. It may distort. It may lead astray. It may be a discord in the tone or symphony. For anybody can act. Most people in England do nothing else. To be conventional is to be a comedian. To act a particular part, however, is a very different thing, and a very difficult thing as well.

Letter to *Daily Telegraph*, 20 February 1892

* * *

* * *

Lord Illingworth: One should never take sides in anything, Mr Kelvil. Taking sides is the beginning of sincerity, and earnestness follows shortly afterwards, and the human being becomes a bore.   *A Woman of No Importance*

Lord Illingworth: The English country gentleman galloping after a fox – the unspeakable in full pursuit of the uneatable.

Lord Illingworth: Twenty years of romance make a woman look like a ruin; but twenty years of marriage make her something like a public building.

Lord Illingworth: One should never trust a woman who tells one her real age. A woman who would tell one that, would tell one anything.

Lord Illingworth: One can survive everything nowadays, except death, and live down anything except a good reputation.

Mrs Allonby: Nothing is so aggravating as calmness.

Mrs Allonby: Men always want to be a woman's first love. That is their clumsy vanity. We women have a more subtle instinct about things. What we like is to be a man's last romance.

Lord Illingworth: Children begin by loving their parents. After a time they judge them. Rarely, if ever, do they forgive them.

Lord Illingworth: If a man is a gentleman, he knows quite enough, and if he is not a gentleman, whatever he knows is bad for him.

Lord Illingworth: ... to the philosopher ... women represent the triumph of matter over mind – just as men represent the triumph of mind over morals.

Lord Illingworth: The history of women is the history of the worst form of tyranny the world has ever known. The tyranny of the weak over the strong. It is the only tyranny that lasts.

Lord Illingworth: Men marry because they are tired; women because they are curious. Both are disappointed.

Lord Illingworth: The only difference between the saint and the sinner is that every saint has a past, and every sinner has a future.

Mrs Allonby: I delight in men over seventy. They always offer one the devotion of a lifetime. I think seventy an ideal age for a man.

* * *

A Few Maxims for the Instruction of the Over-Educated

Education is an admirable thing. But it is well to remember from time to time that nothing that is worth knowing can be taught.

Public opinion exists only where there are no ideas.

The English are always degrading truths into facts. When a truth becomes a fact it loses all its intellectual value.

It is a very sad thing that nowadays there is so little useless information.

The only link between Literature and the Drama left to us in England at the present moment is the bill of the play.

In old days books were written by men of letters and read by the public. Nowadays books are written by the public and read by nobody.

Most women are so artificial that they have no sense of Art. Most men are so natural that they have no sense of Beauty.

Friendship is far more tragic than love. It lasts longer.

What is abnormal in Life stands in normal relations to Art. It is the only thing in Life that stands in normal relations to Art.

A subject that is beautiful in itself gives no suggestion to the artist. It lacks imperfection.

The only thing that the artist cannot see is the obvious. The only thing that the public can see is the obvious. The result is the Criticism of the Journalist.

Art is the only serious thing in the world. And the artist is the only person who is never serious.

To be really medieval one should have no body. To be really modern one should have no soul. To be really Greek one should have no clothes.

Dandyism is the assertion of the absolute modernity of Beauty.

The only thing that can console one for being poor is extravagance. The only thing that can console one for being rich is economy.

One should never listen. To listen is a sign of indifference to one's hearers.

Even the disciple has his uses. He stands behind one's throne, and at the moment of one's triumph whispers in one's ear that, after all, one is immortal.

The criminal classes are so close to us that even the policemen can see them. They are so far away from us that only the poet can understand them.

Those whom the gods love grow young.

*   *   *

Phrases and Philosophies for
the Use of the Young

The first duty in life is to be as artificial as possible. What the second duty is no one has as yet discovered.

Wickedness is a myth invented by good people to account for the curious attractiveness of others.

If the poor only had profiles there would be no difficulty in solving the problem of poverty.

Those who see any difference between soul and body have neither.

A really well-made buttonhole is the only link between Art and Nature.

Religions die when they are proved to be true. Science is the record of dead religions.

The well-bred contradict other people. The wise contradict themselves.

Nothing that actually occurs is of the smallest importance.

Dullness is the coming of age of seriousness.

In all unimportant matters, style, not sincerity, is the essential. In all important matters, style, not sincerity, is the essential.

If one tells the truth, one is sure, sooner or later, to be found out.

Pleasure is the only thing one should live for. Nothing ages like happiness.

It is only by not paying one's bills that one can hope to live in the memory of the commercial classes.

No crime is vulgar, but all vulgarity is crime. Vulgarity is the conduct of others.

Only the shallow know themselves.

Time is waste of money.

One should always be a little improbable.

There is a fatality about all good resolutions. They are invariably made too soon.

The only way to atone for being occasionally a little over-dressed is by being always absolutely over-educated.

To be premature is to be perfect.

Any preoccupation with ideas of what is right or wrong in conduct shows an arrested intellectual development.

Ambition is the last refuge of the failure.

A truth ceases to be true when more than one person believes in it.

In examinations the foolish ask questions that the wise cannot answer.

Greek dress was in its essence inartistic. Nothing should reveal the body but the body.

One should either be a work of art, or wear a work of art.

It is only the superficial qualities that last. Man's deeper nature is soon found out.

Industry is the root of all ugliness.

The ages live in history through their anachronisms.

It is only the gods who taste of death. Apollo has passed away, but Hyacinth, whom men say he slew, lives on. Nero and Narcissus are always with us.

The old believe everything: the middle-aged suspect everything: the young know everything.

The condition of perfection is idleness: the aim of perfection is youth.

Only the great masters of style ever succeed in being obscure.

There is something tragic about the enormous number of young men there are in England at the present moment who start life with perfect profiles, and end by adopting some useful profession.

To love oneself is the beginning of a life-long romance.

* * *

* * *

Mrs Cheveley: Ah! the strength of women comes from the fact that psychology cannot explain us. Men can be analysed, women . . . merely adored.   *An Ideal Husband*

Lord Goring: . . . it is a very dangerous thing to listen. If one listens one may be convinced; and a man who allows himself to be convinced by an argument is a thoroughly unreasonable person.

Lady Markby: . . . I think anything is better than high intellectual pressure. That is the most unbecoming thing there is. It makes the noses of the young girls so particularly large. And there is nothing so difficult to marry as a large nose; men don't like them.

Lady Chiltern: One's past is what one is. It is the only way by which people should be judged.

Lord Goring: . . . no man should have a secret from his own wife. She invariably finds it out. Women have a wonderful instinct about things. They can discover everything except the obvious.

Lord Goring: There is more to be said for stupidity than people imagine. Personally I have a great admiration for stupidity. It is a sort of fellow-feeling, I suppose.

Sir Robert Chiltern: ... when the gods wish to punish us they answer our prayers.

Lord Goring: ... I usually say what I really think. A great mistake nowadays. It makes one so liable to be misunderstood.

Lord Goring: ... in England a man who can't talk morality twice a week to a large, popular, immoral audience is quite over as a serious politician.

Lady Markby: Nothing is so dangerous as being too modern. One is apt to grow old-fashioned quite suddenly.

Mrs Cheveley: The art of living. The only really Fine Art we have produced in modern times.

Lady Markby: ... nothing ages a woman so rapidly as having married the general rule.

Mrs Cheveley: Morality is simply the attitude we adopt towards people whom we personally dislike.

Lord Goring: You see, Phipps, Fashion is what one wears oneself. What is unfashionable is what other people wear.

Phipps: Yes, my lord.

Lord Goring: Just as vulgarity is simply the conduct of other people.

Phipps: Yes, my lord.

Lord Goring: And falsehoods the truths of other people.

Phipps: Yes, my lord.

Lord Goring: Other people are quite dreadful. The only possible society is oneself.

Phipps: Yes, my lord.

Lord Goring: To love oneself is the beginning of a life-long romance, Phipps.

Phipps: Yes, my lord.

Lord Goring: It is the growth of the moral sense in women that makes marriage such a hopeless, one-sided institution.

Mrs Cheveley: One should never give a woman anything that she can't wear in the evening.

Mrs Cheveley: ... women are never disarmed by compliments. Men always are. That is the difference between the two sexes.

Mrs Cheveley: Oh, there is only one real tragedy in a woman's life. The fact that her past is always her lover, and her future invariably her husband.

Lord Goring: Fathers should be neither seen nor heard. That is the only proper basis for family life.

Lord Goring: ... only people who look dull ever get into the House of Commons, and only people who are dull ever succeed there.

* * *

As the cross-examination proceeded, it became clear that Wilde was retorting cavalierly to Carson's questions. Instead of expounding his theory of art as an enhancement and expansion of life, he presented himself as amoral artist and scorned the moral mob. Early in the prosecution case, as Ralph Hodgson recalled, Carson read a passage from

Dorian Gray, and demanded, 'Did you write that?' Wilde said he had the honor to be the author. Carson laid down the book with a sneer and turned over some papers. Wilde was lost in thought. Presently Carson read aloud a piece of verse from one of Wilde's articles, 'And I suppose you wrote that also, Mr Wilde?' Wilde waited till you could hear a pin drop and then said, very quietly, 'Ah no, Mr Carson, Shakespeare wrote that.' Carson went scarlet. He turned pages again and read another piece of verse and said, 'And I suppose Shakespeare wrote that also, Mr Wilde?' 'Not as you read it, Mr Carson,' Oscar said. The judge said he would clear the court if there was more noise. Wilde deliberately turned his back, folded his arms, and looked far away through the ceiling in rapt concentration. It was effectively done. Carson thundered at him to conduct himself properly: and he appealed to the judge, 'M'lud, M'lud.' Wilde stared deeper into the void for a full minute. Suddenly he swung round as if he heard Carson for the first time and said, assuming a most apologetic tone, 'I beg your pardon, Mr Carson; I do beg your pardon.' When Carson suggested that *Dorian Gray* was perverted, Wilde replied, 'That could only be to brutes and illiterates. The views of Philistines on art are incalculably stupid.'   Quoted in Ellmann (from Wilde's libel suit against
the 10th Marquess of Queensberry)

*   *   *

* * *

The 'Love that dare not speak its name' in this century is such a great affection of an elder for a younger man as there was between David and Jonathan, such as Plato made the very basis of his philosophy, and such as you find in the sonnets of Michaelangelo and Shakespeare. It is that deep, spiritual affection that is as pure as it is perfect. It dictates and pervades great works of art like those of Shakespeare and Michaelangelo, and those two letters of mine, such as they are. It is in this century misunderstood, so much misunderstood that it may be described as the 'Love that dare not speak its name', and on account of it I am placed where I am now. It is beautiful, it is fine, it is the noblest form of affection. There is nothing unnatural about it. It is intellectual, and it repeatedly exists between an elder and a younger man, when the elder man has intellect, and the younger man has all the joy, hope and glamour of life before him. That it should be so the world does not understand. The world mocks at it and sometimes puts one in the pillory for it.

Quoted in Ellmann (from Wilde's first trial,
Regina v. *Wilde and Taylor*, 30 April 1895)

* * *

* * *

Oh, it is indeed a burning shame that there would be one law for men and another law for women. I think that there should be no law for anybody.   *Sketch*, 9 January 1895

* * *

After the first glass, you see things as you wish they were. After the second, you see things as they are not. Finally you see things as they really are, and that is the most horrible thing in the world.   (On absinthe)

* * *

My existence is a scandal.
(Attrib.)

* * *

* * *

Lane: I have only been married once. That was in consequence of a misunderstanding between myself and a young person.   *The Importance of Being Earnest*

Algernon: The truth is rarely pure and never simple. Modern life would be very tedious if it were either, and modern literature a complete impossibility.

Algernon: The amount of women in London who flirt with their own husbands is perfectly scandalous. It looks so bad. It is simply washing one's clean linen in public.

Lady Bracknell: Ignorance is like a delicate exotic fruit; touch it and the bloom is gone. The whole theory of modern education is radically unsound. Fortunately in England, at any rate, education produces no effect whatsoever. If it did, it would prove a serious danger to the upper classes, and probably lead to acts of violence in Grosvenor Square.

Lady Bracknell: To lose one parent, Mr Worthing, may be regarded as a misfortune; to lose both looks like carelessness.

Lady Bracknell: Mr Worthing, I confess I feel somewhat bewildered by what you have just told me. To be born, or at any rate bred, in a hand-bag, whether it had handles or not, seems to me to display a contempt for the ordinary decencies of family life that reminds one of the worst excesses of the French Revolution. And I presume you know what that unfortunate movement led to? As for the particular locality in which the hand-bag was found, a cloak-room at a railway station might serve to conceal a social indiscretion – has probably, indeed, been used for that purpose before now – but it could hardly be regarded as an assured basis for a recognized position in good society.

Algernon: Relations are simply a tedious pack of people, who haven't got the remotest knowledge of how to live, nor the smallest instinct about when to die.

Algernon: All women become like their mothers. That is their tragedy. No man does. That's his.

Algernon: The only way to behave to a woman is to make love to her, if she is pretty, and to someone else, if she is plain.

Miss Prism: No married man is ever attractive except to his wife.

Chasuble: And often, I've been told, not even to her.

Miss Prism: That depends on the intellectual sympathies of the woman. Maturity can always be depended on. Ripeness can be trusted. Young women are green. I spoke horticulturally. My metaphor was drawn from fruits.

Algernon: If I am occasionally a little over-dressed, I make up for it by being always immensely over-educated.

Algernon: It is very vulgar to talk about one's business. Only people like stockbrokers do that, and then merely at dinner parties.

Lady Bracknell: I am not in favour of long engagements. They give people the opportunity of finding out each other's character before marriage, which I think is never advisable.

Lady Bracknell: I dislike arguments of any kind. They are always vulgar, and often convincing.

* * *

* * *

It often happens that the real tragedies of life occur in such an inarticulate manner that they hurt one by their crude violence, their absolute incoherence, their absurd want of meaning, their entire lack of style.   Quoted in Ellmann

* * *

Excerpts from
The Ballad of Reading Gaol

In Memoriam
C.T.W.
Sometime Trooper of the Royal Horse Guards.
Obiit H. M. Prison; Reading, Berkshire
July 7th, 1896

Yet each man kills the thing he loves,
  By each let this be heard,
Some do it with a bitter look,
  Some with a flattering word,
The coward does it with a kiss,
  The brave man with a sword!

Some kill their love when they are young,
  And some when they are old;
Some strangle with the hands of Lust,
  Some with the hands of Gold:
The kindest use a knife, because
  The dead so soon grow cold.

Some love too little, some too long,
  Some sell, and others buy;
Some do the deed with many tears,
  And some without a sigh:
For each man kills the thing he loves,
  Yet each man does not die.

With sudden shock the prison-clock
   Smote on the shivering air,
And from all the gaol rose up a wail
   Of impotent despair,
Like the sound that frightened marshes hear
   From some leper in his lair.

And as one sees most fearful things
   In the crystal of a dream,
We saw the greasy hempen rope
   Hooked to the blackened beam,
And heard the prayer the hangman's snare
   Strangled into a scream.

And all the woe that moved him so
   That he gave that bitter cry,
And the wild regrets, and bloody sweats,
   None knew so well as I:
For he who lives more lives than one
   More deaths than one must die.

*

I know not whether Laws be right,
   Or whether Laws be wrong;
All that we know who lie in gaol
   Is that the wall is strong;
And that each day is like a year,
   A year whose days are long.

But this I know, that every Law
   That men have made for Man,
Since first Man took his brother's life,
   And the sad world began,
But straws the wheat and saves the chaff
   With a most evil fan.

This too I know — and wise it were
   If each could know the same —
That every prison that men build
   Is built with bricks of shame,
And bound with bars lest Christ should see
   How men their brothers maim.

With bars they blur the gracious moon,
   And blind the goodly sun:
And they do well to hide their Hell,
   For in it things are done
That Son of God nor son of Man
   Ever should look upon!

*

The vilest deeds like poison weeds
    Bloom well in prison-air:
It is only what is good in Man
    That wastes and withers there:
Pale Anguish keeps the heavy gate,
    And the Warder is Despair.

For they starve the little frightened child
    Till it weeps both night and day:
And they scourge the weak, and flog the fool,
    And gibe the old and gray,
And some grow mad, and all grow bad,
    And none a word may say.

Each narrow cell in which we dwell
    Is a foul and dark latrine.
And fetid breath of living Death
    Chokes up each grated screen,
And all, but Lust, is turned to dust
    In Humanity's machine.

The brackish water that we drink
    Creeps with a loathsome slime,
And the bitter bread they weigh in scales
    Is full of chalk and lime,
And Sleep will not lie down, but walks
    Wild-eyed, and cries to Time.

*

In Reading gaol by Reading town
    There is a pit of shame,
And in it lies a wretched man
    Eaten by teeth of flame,
In a burning winding-sheet he lies,
    And his grave has got no name.

And there, till Christ call forth the dead,
    In silence let him lie:
No need to waste the foolish tear,
    Or heave the windy sigh:
The man had killed the thing he loved,
    And so he had to die.

And all men kill the thing they love,
    By all let this be heard,
Some do it with a bitter look,
    Some with a flattering word,
The coward does it with a kiss,
    The brave man with a sword!

* * *

* * *

Sphinx, how marvellous of you to know exactly the right hat to wear at seven o'clock in the morning to meet a friend who has been away!

> Oscar Wilde, to Mrs Leverson, on his leaving prison,
> 1897 (Attrib.)

* * *

The real fool ... is he who does not know himself ... The supreme vice is shallowness.   *De Profundis*

Nothing really at any period of my life was ever of the smallest importance to me compared with Art. But in the case of an artist, weakness is nothing less than a crime, when it is a weakness that paralyses the imagination.

The basis of character is will power ...

Ultimately the bond of all companionship, whether in marriage or in friendship, is conversation ...

Sins of the flesh are nothing. They are maladies for physicians to cure, if they should be cured. Sins of the soul alone are shameful.

The aim of love is to love: no more, and no less.

All homage is delightful to an artist and doubly sweet when youth brings it.

Prosperity, pleasure and success, may be rough of grain and common in fibre, but sorrow is the most sensitive of all created things. There is nothing that stirs in the whole world of thought to which sorrow does not vibrate in terrible and exquisite pulsation.

I was a man who stood in symbolic relations to the art and culture of my age ... Few men hold such a position in their own lifetime, and have it so acknowledged.

I had genius, a distinguished name, high social position, brilliancy, intellectual daring; I made art a philosophy and philosophy an art; I altered the minds of men and the colours of things; there was nothing I said or did that did not make people wonder. I took the drama, the most objective form known to art, and made it as personal a mode of expression as the lyric or sonnet; at the same time I widened its range and enriched its characterization. Drama, novel, poem in prose, poem in rhyme, subtle or fantastic dialogue, whatever I touched, I made beautiful in a new mode of beauty: to truth itself I gave what is false no less than what is true as its rightful province, and showed that the false and the true are merely forms of intellectual existence. I treated art as the supreme reality and life as a mere mode of fiction. I awoke the imagination of my century so that it created myth and legend around me. I summed up all systems in a phrase and all existence in an epigram. Along with these things I had things that were different. But I let myself be lured into long spells of senseless and sensual ease. I amused myself with being a *flâneur*, a dandy, a man of fashion. I surrounded myself with the smaller natures and the meaner minds. I became the spendthrift of my own genius, and to waste an eternal youth gave me a curious joy. Tired of being on the heights, I deliberately went to the depths in the search for new sensation. What the paradox was to me in the sphere of thought, perversity became to me in the sphere of passion. Desire, at the end, was a malady, or a madness, or both. I grew careless of the lives of others. I took pleasure where it pleased me, and passed on. I forgot that every little action of the common day makes or unmakes character, and that therefore what one has done in the secret chamber one has some day to cry aloud on the house-tops. I ceased to be lord over myself. I was no longer the captain of my soul, and did not know it. I allowed pleasure to dominate me. I ended in horrible disgrace.

Religion does not help me. The faith that others give to what is unseen, I give to what one can touch, and look at. My gods dwell in temples made with hands; and within the circle of actual experience is my creed made perfect and complete.

To regret one's own experiences is to arrest one's own development. To deny one's own experiences is to put a lie into the lips of one's own life. It is no less than a denial of the soul.

What the artist is always looking for is the mode of existence in which soul and body are one and indivisible: in which the outward is expressive of the inward: in which form reveals.

Now it seems to me that love of some kind is the only possible explanation of the extraordinary amount of suffering that there is in the world.

Most people are other people. Their thoughts are someone else's opinions, their lives a mimicry, their passions a quotation.

Every single work of art is the fulfilment of a prophecy: for every work of art is the conversion of an idea into an image.

... all great ideas are dangerous.

Art only begins where Imitation ends ...

All bad art is the result of good intentions.

* * *

Further Reading

(*The place of publication is London unless otherwise stated*)

Oscar Wilde, *Complete Short Fiction*, ed. Ian Small (Penguin, 1994)

Oscar Wilde, *De Profundis and Other Writings* (Penguin, 1954)

Oscar Wilde, *The Importance of Being Earnest and Other Plays* (Penguin, 1986)

Oscar Wilde, *The Picture of Dorian Gray*, ed. Peter Ackroyd (Penguin, 1985)

The Letters of Oscar Wilde, ed. Rupert Hart-Davies (John Murray, 1962)

More Letters of Oscar Wilde, ed. Rupert Hart-Davis (John Murray, 1985)

The Best of Oscar Wilde, ed. Robert Pearce (Duckworth, 1997)

The Fireworks of Oscar Wilde, ed. Owen Dudley Edwards (Barrie & Jenkins, 1989)

I Can Resist Everything Except Temptation, ed. Karl Beckson (Columbia University Press, New York, 1996)

Oscar Wilde, Selected Poems, ed. Robert Mighall (Everyman, 1996)

The Uncollected Oscar Wilde, ed. John Wyse Jackson (Fourth Estate, 1991)

Richard Ellmann, *Oscar Wilde* (Hamish Hamilton, 1987; Penguin, 1988)